Sam Hart

The Love Language of Dogs

Illustrations by
Tatiana Davidova

Hilarious Ways Your Dog is Trying to Show Their Love

summersdale

THE LOVE LANGUAGE OF DOGS

Text by Annie Fay Meitchik

Illustrations by Tatiana Davidova

An Hachette UK Company
www.hachette.co.uk

Summersdale Publishers
Part of Octopus Publishing Group Limited
Carmelite House
50 Victoria Embankment
LONDON
EC4Y 0DZ
UK

www.summersdale.com

The authorized representative in the EEA is Hachette Ireland, 8 Castlecourt Centre, Dublin 15, D15 XTP3, Ireland (email: info@hbgi.ie)

Printed and bound in China

ISBN: 978-1-83799-651-3

This FSC® label means that materials used for the product have been responsibly sourced

Substantial discounts on bulk quantities of Summersdale books are available to corporations, professional associations and other organizations. For details contact general enquiries: telephone: +44 (0) 1243 771107 or email: enquiries@summersdale.com.

Introduction

Cuddly, affectionate, loyal and, well, sometimes misguided, the sweet pups in our lives try to win our hearts in unusual ways. Each day, dogs wake up with a mission to bring smiles to the world around them. But, even with the best of intentions, things don't always go as paw-fectly as they might hope. In this book, we'll explore some of the ways your pet may doggedly try to express their love.

Sometimes treasure
is hidden in plain sight.
Your dog only wants to
share that joy with you!

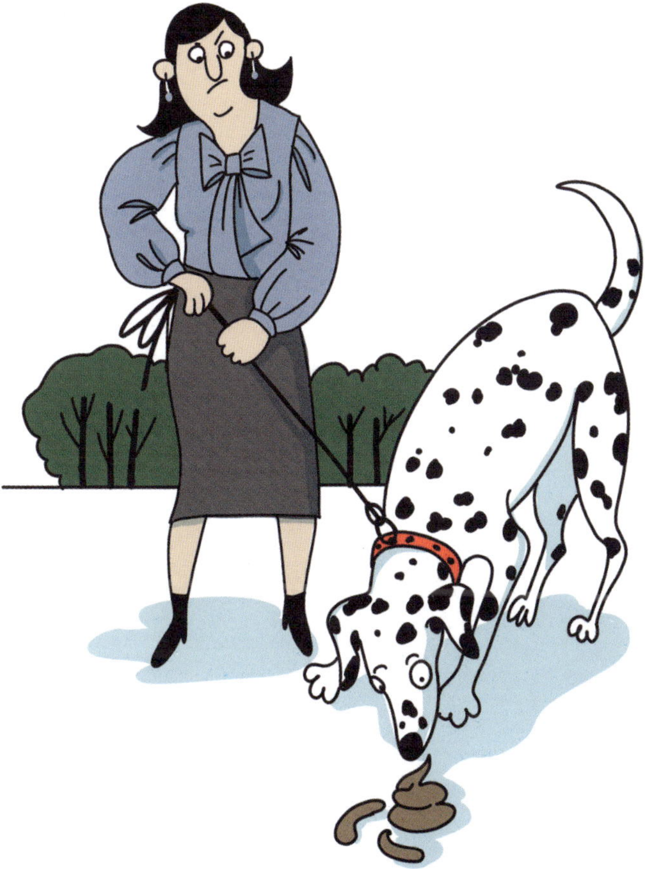

You may not think
there's much to admire
about the view on your
local dog walk, but dogs
have a way of helping
you slow down to
appreciate nature.

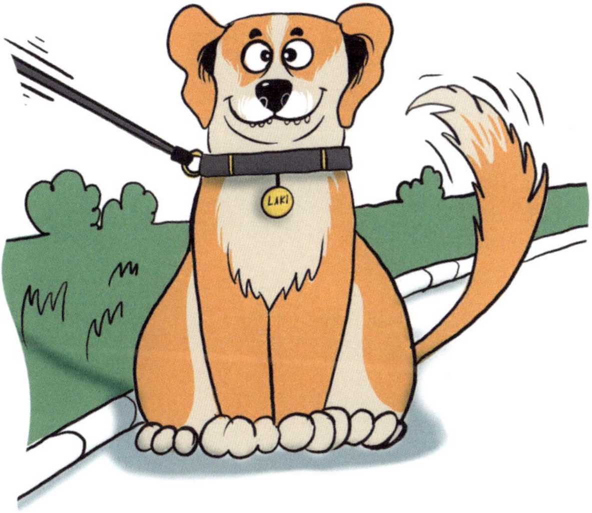
LAKI

When you're hoping
to wind down, your dog will
recommend putting on a
nice, relaxing mud mask.

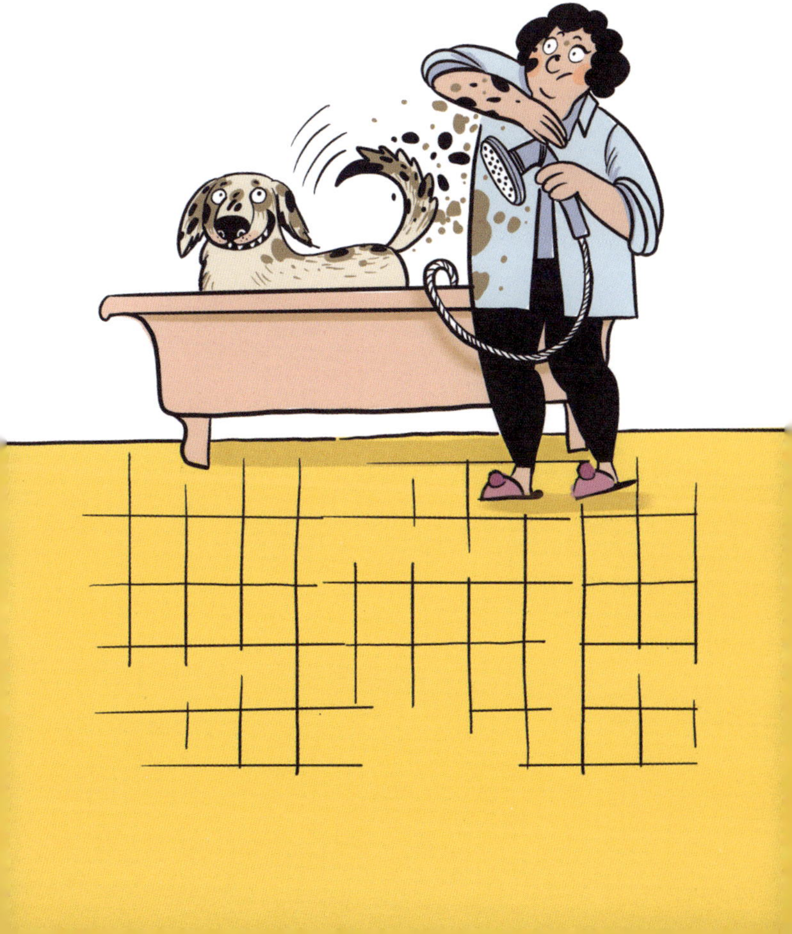

When they think you're in the mood to do something fun, dogs are happy to take the lead and plan a spontaneous date.

Dogs understand that interior designers are expensive, so they're keen to help you redecorate for free.

Rest assured, your
dog will protect you
from all kinds of
potential dangers.

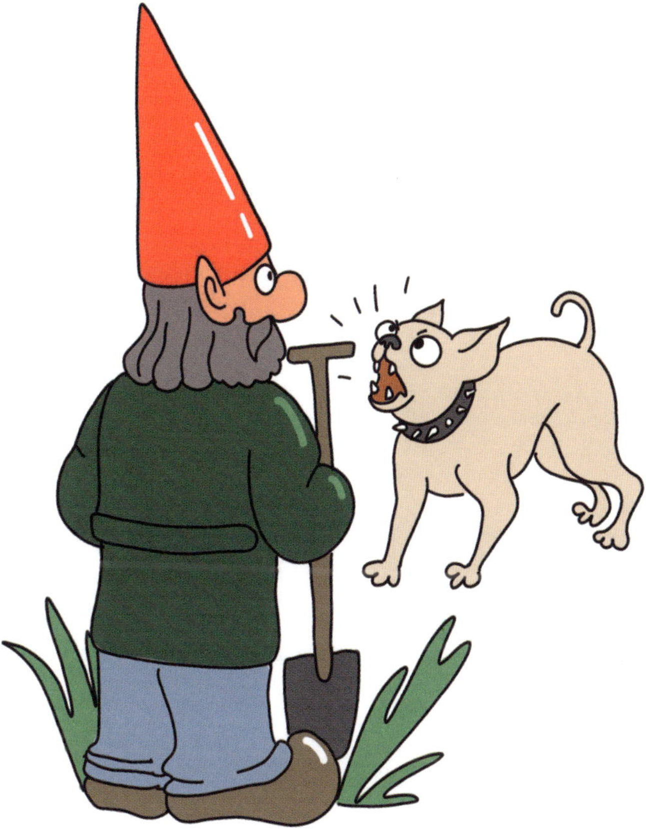

Your pup doesn't want to create extra work for you, so they'll help themselves to some water to save you the trouble.

Known to wear fur coats year-round, your dog will help you make bold style choices, too.

Your dog will always
make sure your
flowers are smelling
nice and fragrant.

Dogs make amazing gift givers.

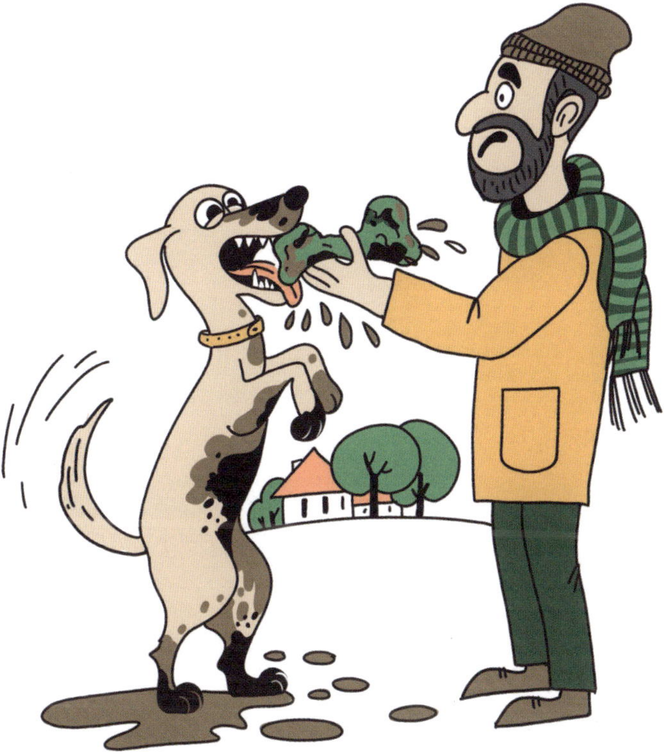

They're equally amazing at keeping gifts and valuable items safe for you.

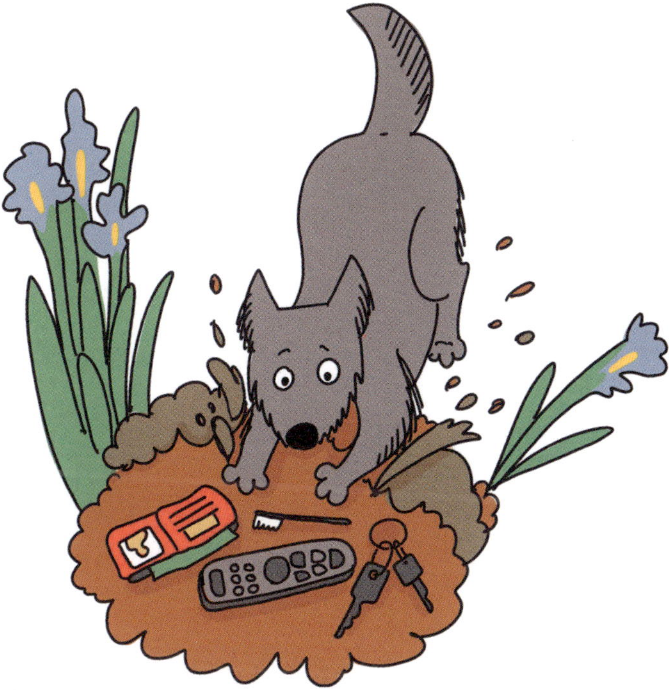

No matter how many cosy alternatives you present your dog with, they will never pass up an opportunity to cuddle with you.

Your puppy will
remind you of the
simple pleasures in
life, like the wonderful
feeling of fresh air
on your face.

**Dogs have a knack
for picking up on their
humans' needs.**

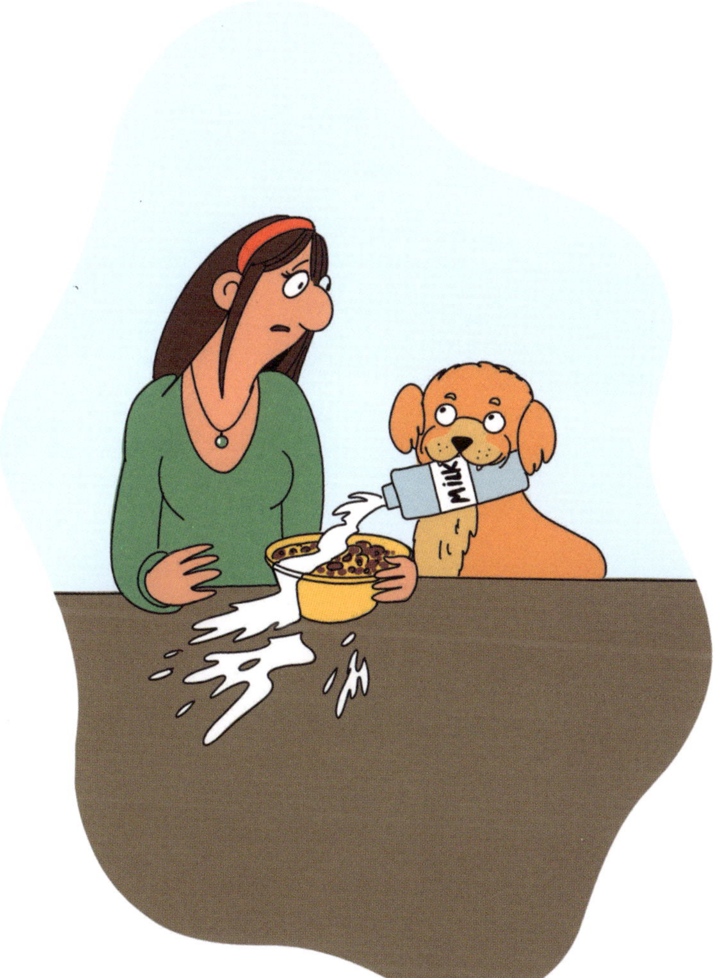
MILK

Nobody enjoys chores,
but your puppy
is always happy to
clean the dishes.

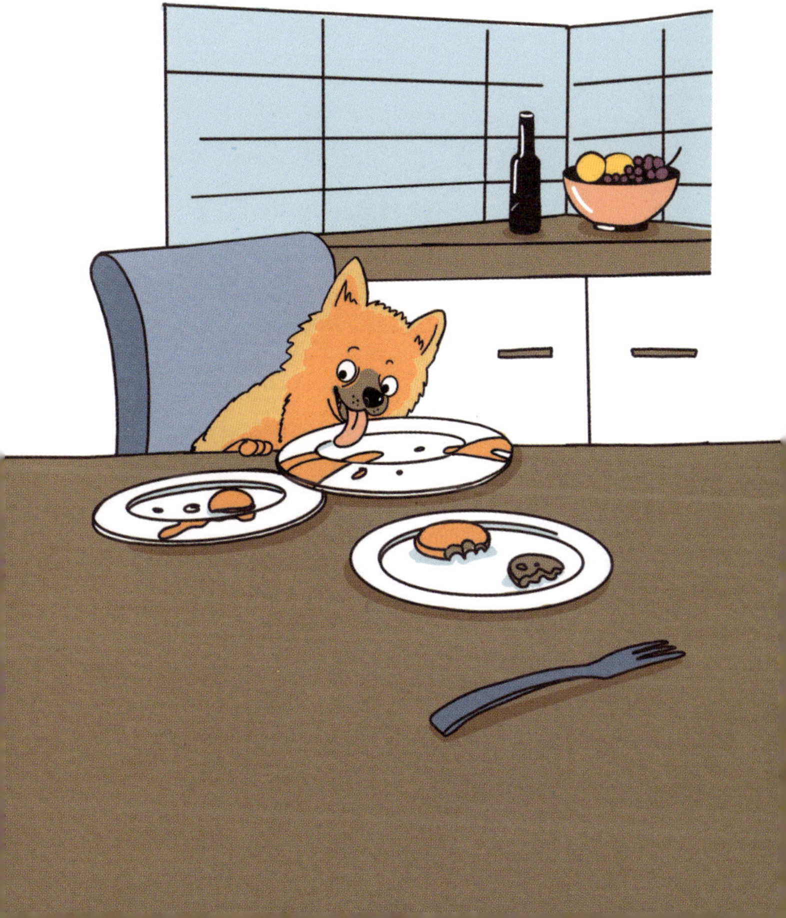

Your dog may even
help you take out the trash
from time to time.

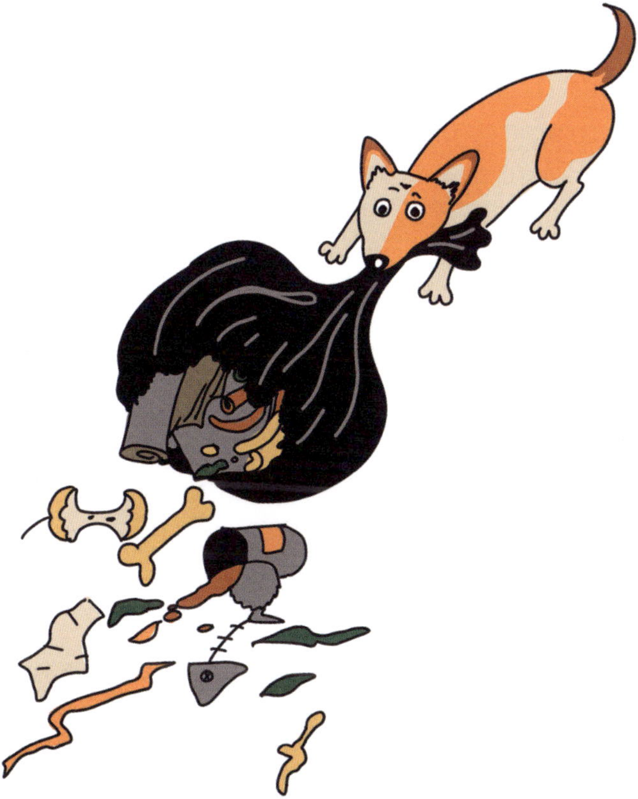

**When it comes
to laundry, dogs love
to help organize!**

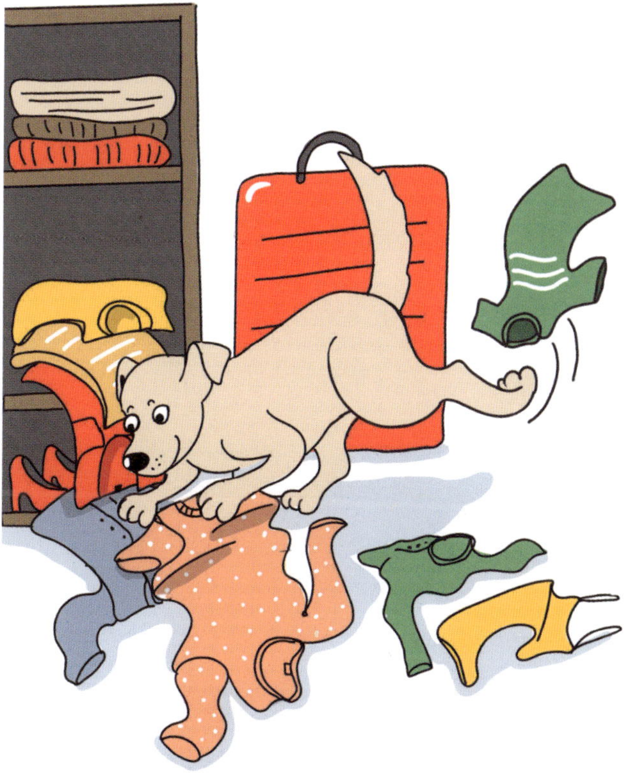

It's common knowledge
that a dog's love
knows no bounds.

Your dog will do
their absolute best to
sing "Happy Birthday"
to you louder than
anyone else.

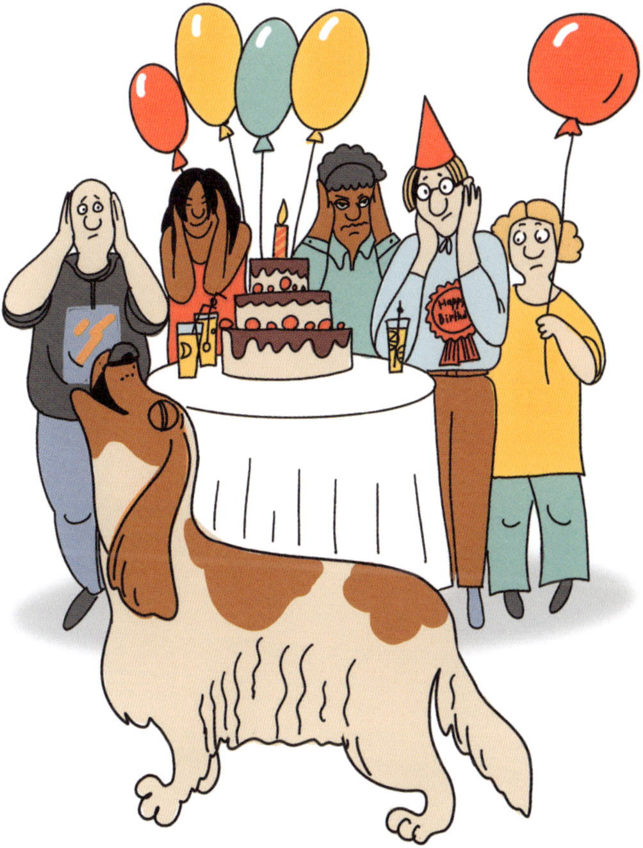

Don't be surprised
if they want to cook
dinner for you but get a
little sidetracked while
preparing the ingredients.

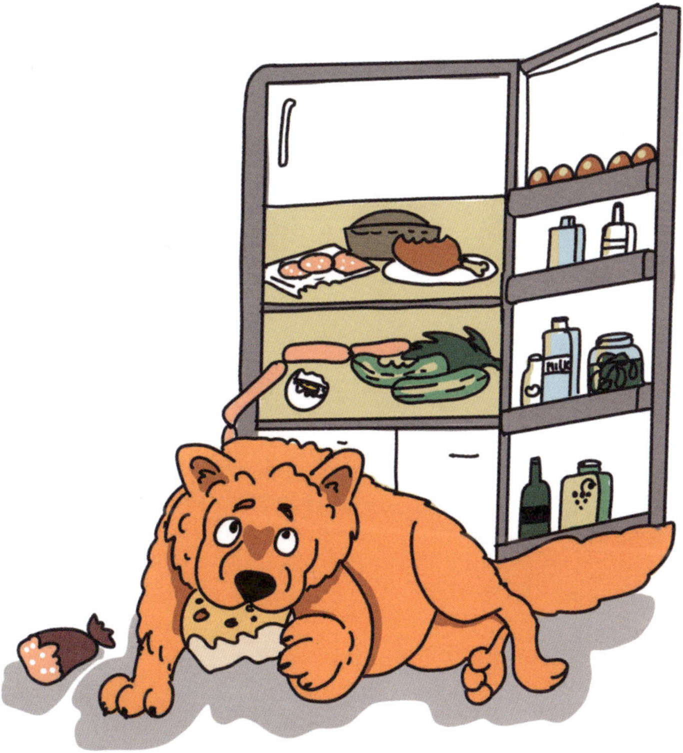
MILK

In a bid to impress you
and your colleagues, your
dog may interpret the phrase
"Zoom call" a little too literally.

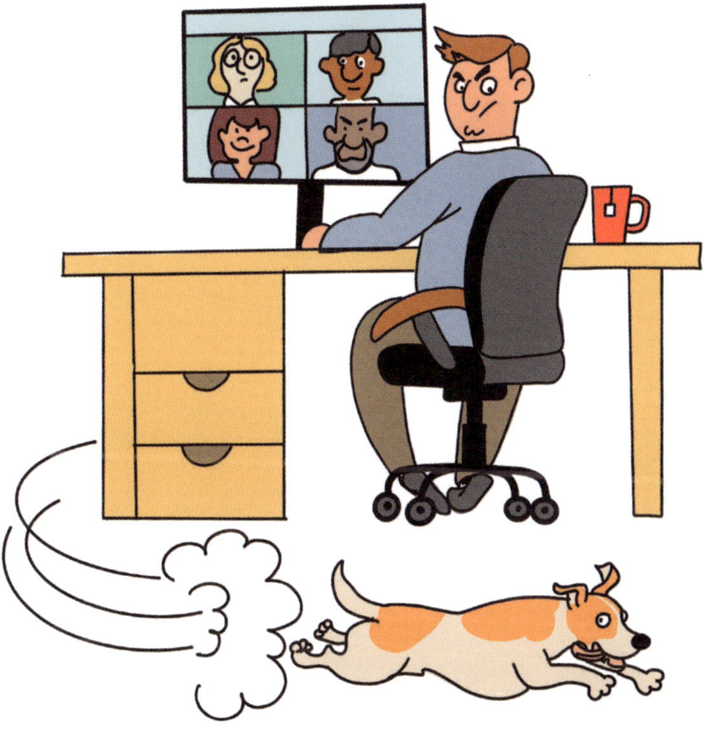

Dogs are very generous;
they will try to give you
free things all the time.

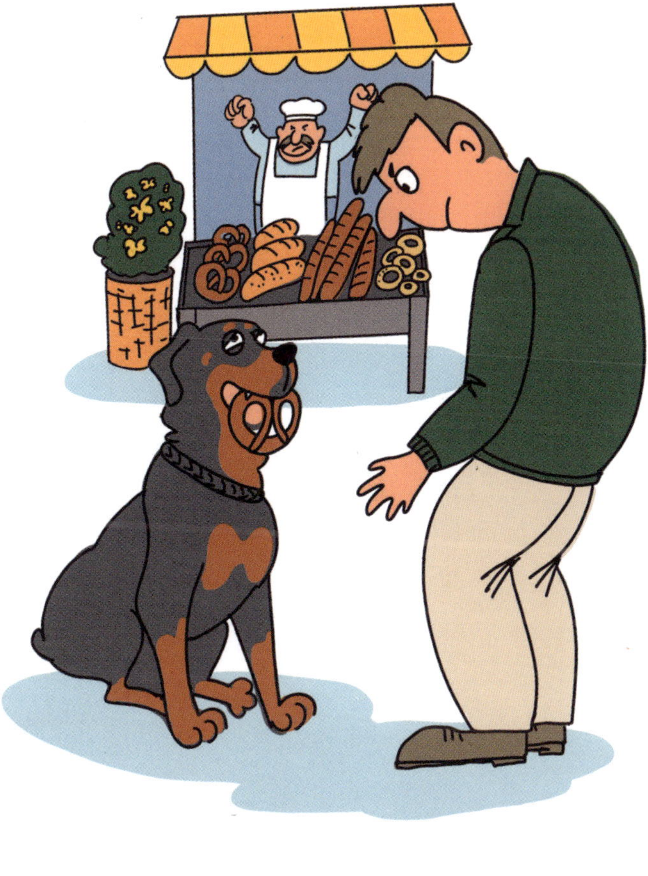

Your puppy wants to help
you make new friends,
but they forget that it's
always them who winds up
getting all the attention.

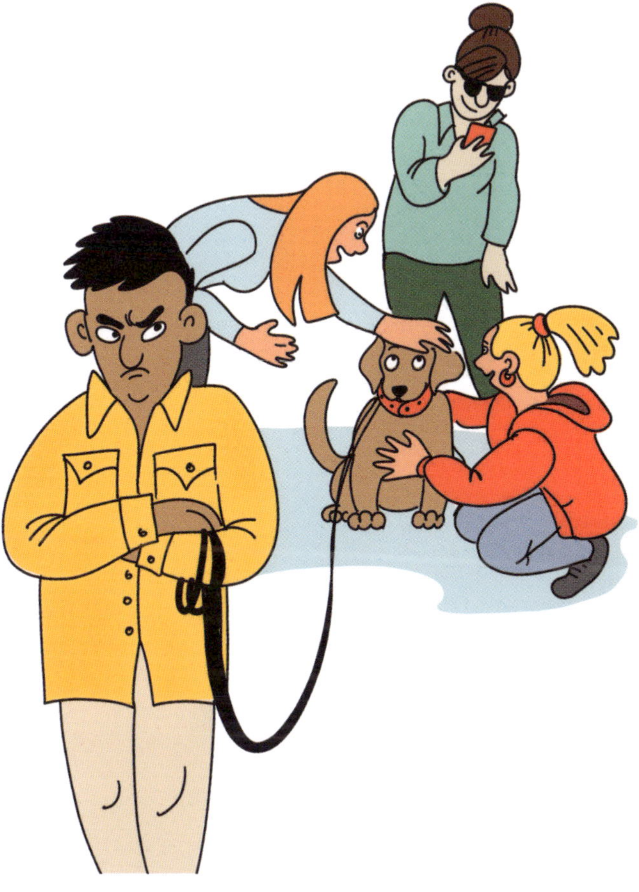

Your dog may want to impress
you by learning new tricks,
but be careful about teaching
them to "roll over".

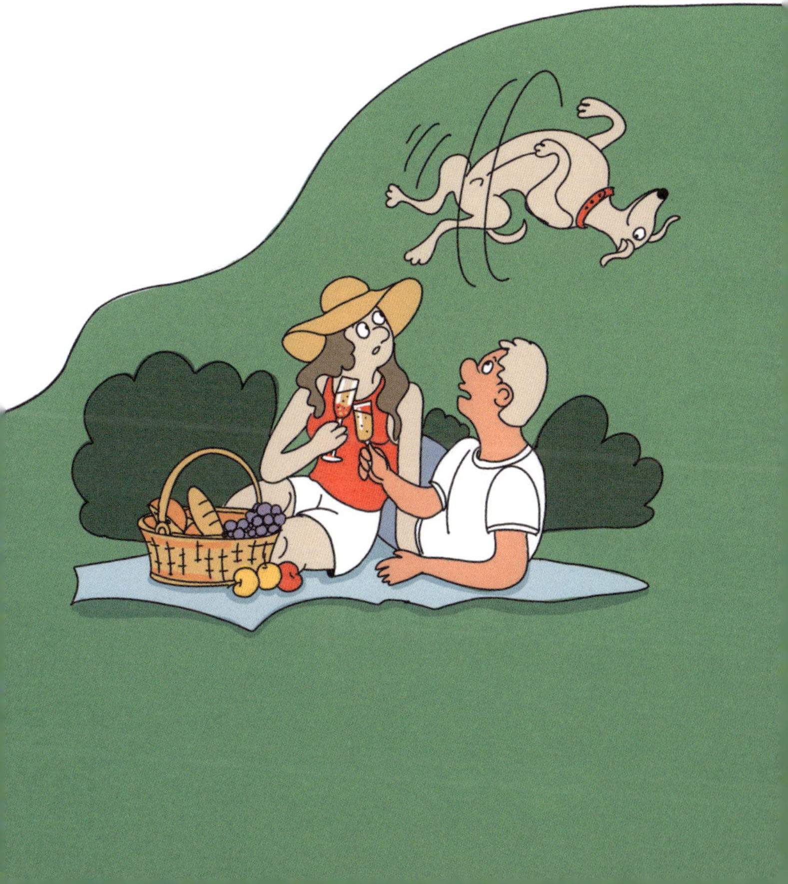

Hoping to impress
your guests? Your dog
will be more than happy
to welcome them
on your behalf.

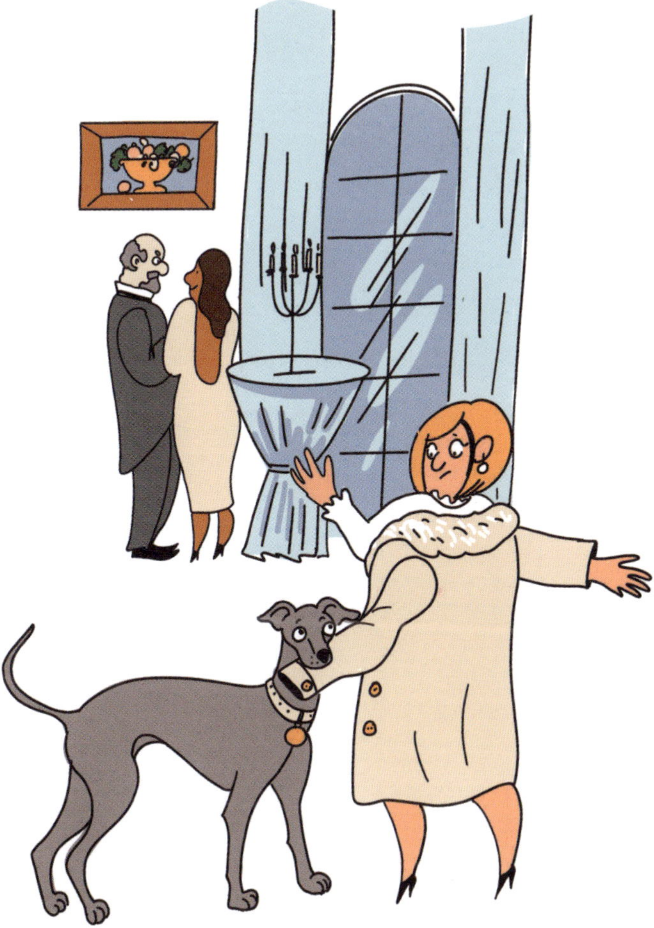

If you're looking
a little sluggish,
your dog will ensure
you're refreshed and
re-energized in no time.

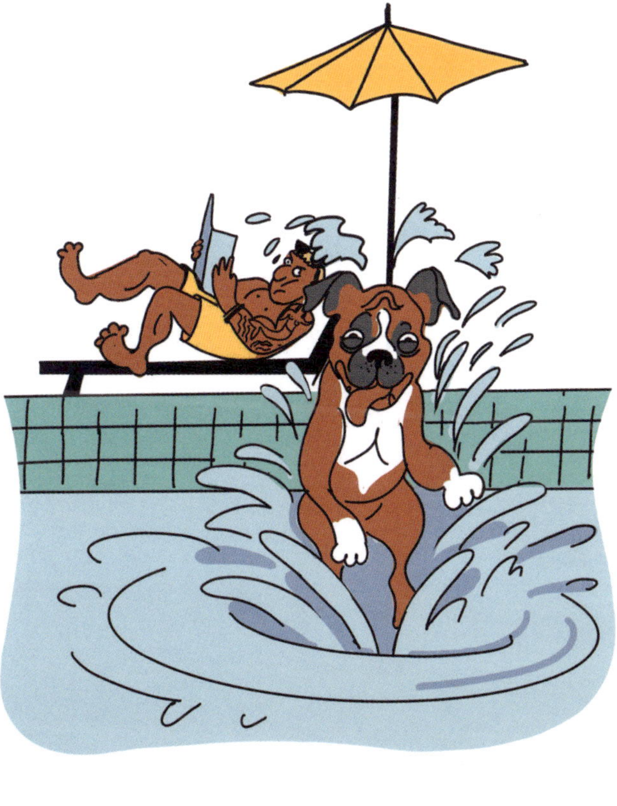

They can show you how
to source organic groceries
without even taking a trip
to the farmer's market.

Your dog loves a good bonding session but can't always tell when they're third wheeling.

Your dog will be happy
to offer you a quick smell
check before you head out
of the house, whether
you ask them to or not.

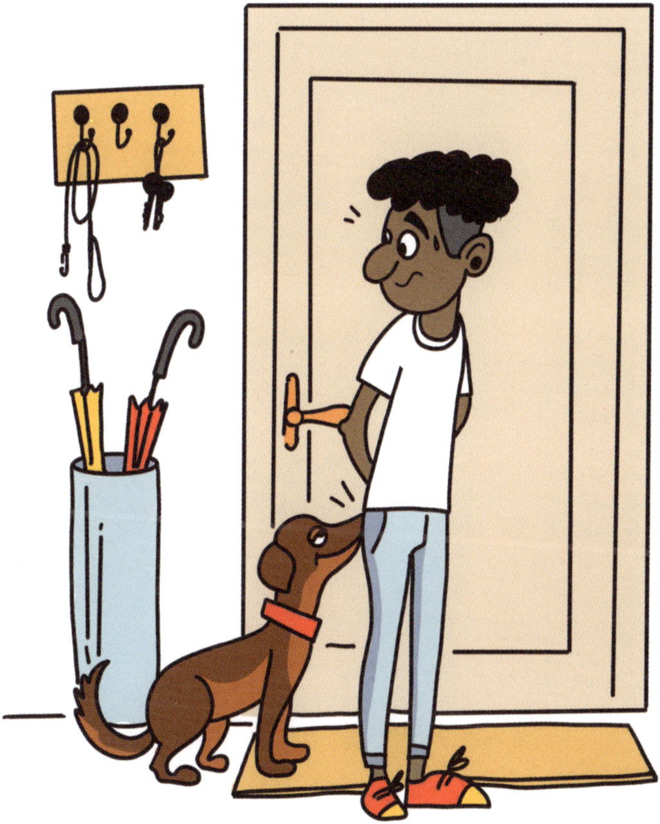

Hypo-allergenic?
Your dog thought you
wanted "hyper".

Feeling chilly?
Your fluffy friend
is here to help!

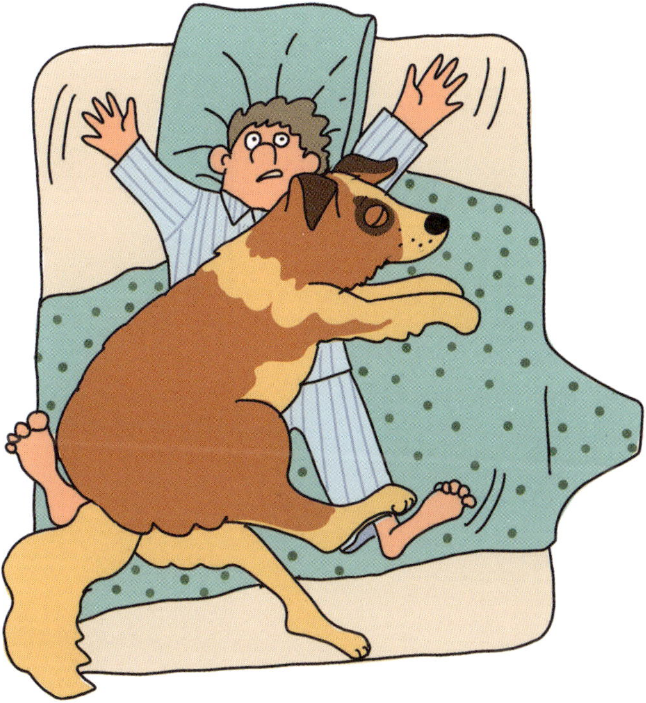

With their excellent
sense of smell, your dog
can help you to clear any
out-of-date products
from your fridge.

When they make mistakes, dogs are quick to show their remorse.

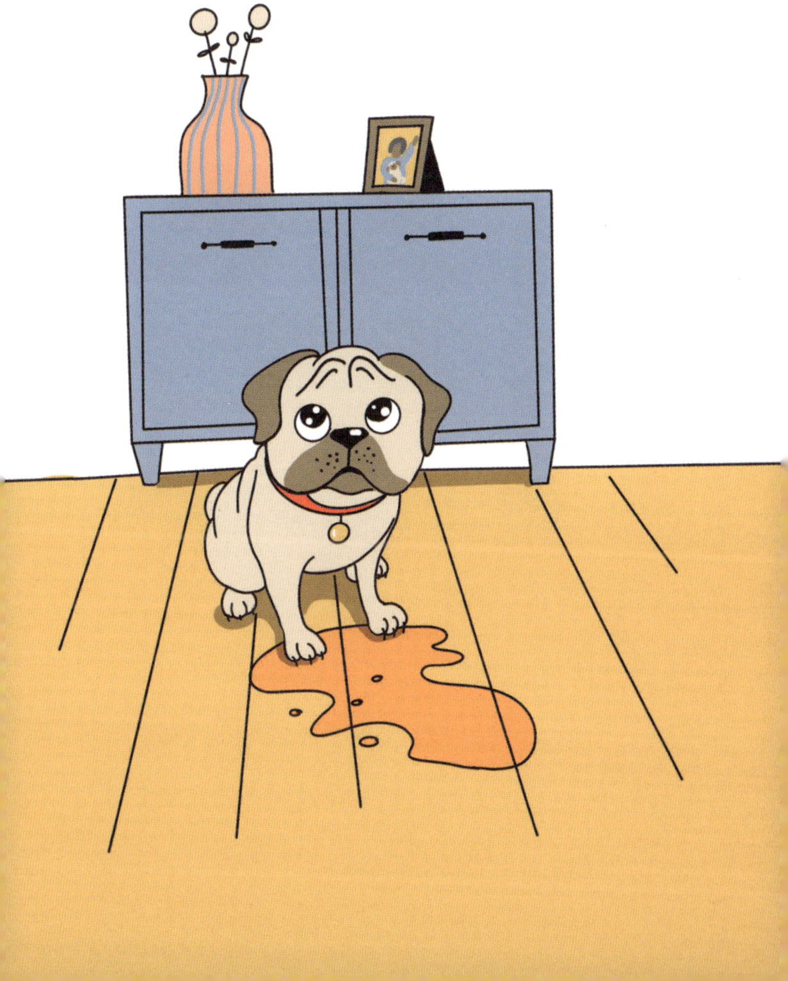

On summer days,
your dog might take it
upon themselves to
help you cool off.

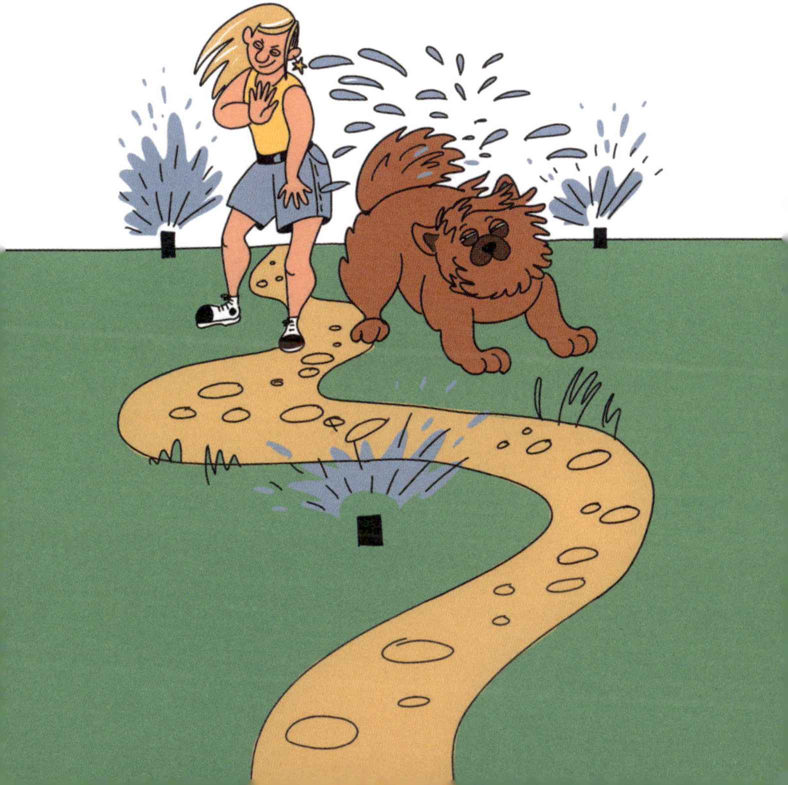

Your furry friend might want to serenade you on a full moon. How magical!

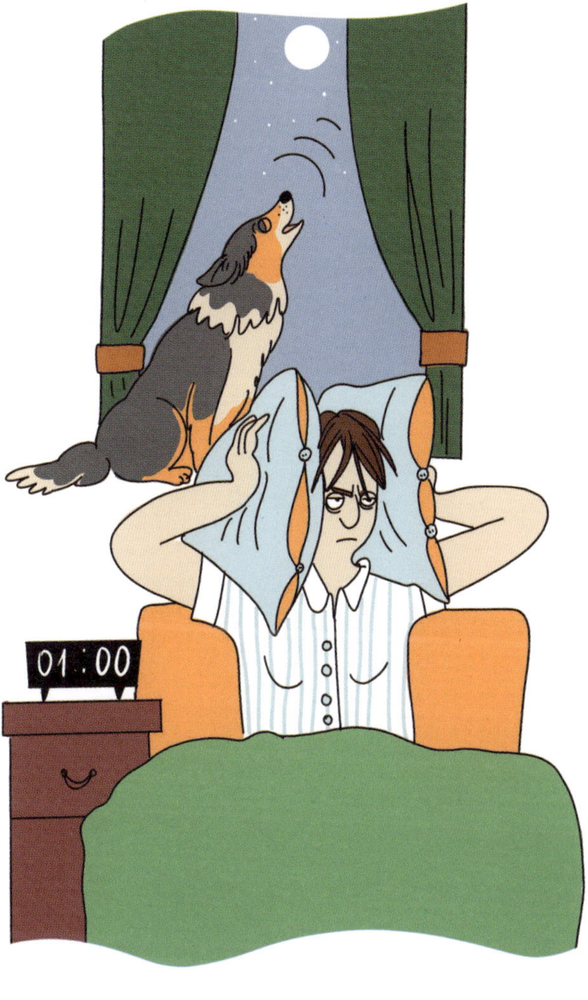
01:00

When it comes to
getting ready, your dog
will go to great lengths
to help you save time.

Dogs know how important sleep is, so they make an effort to show you that it's okay to rest... no matter when or where you are.

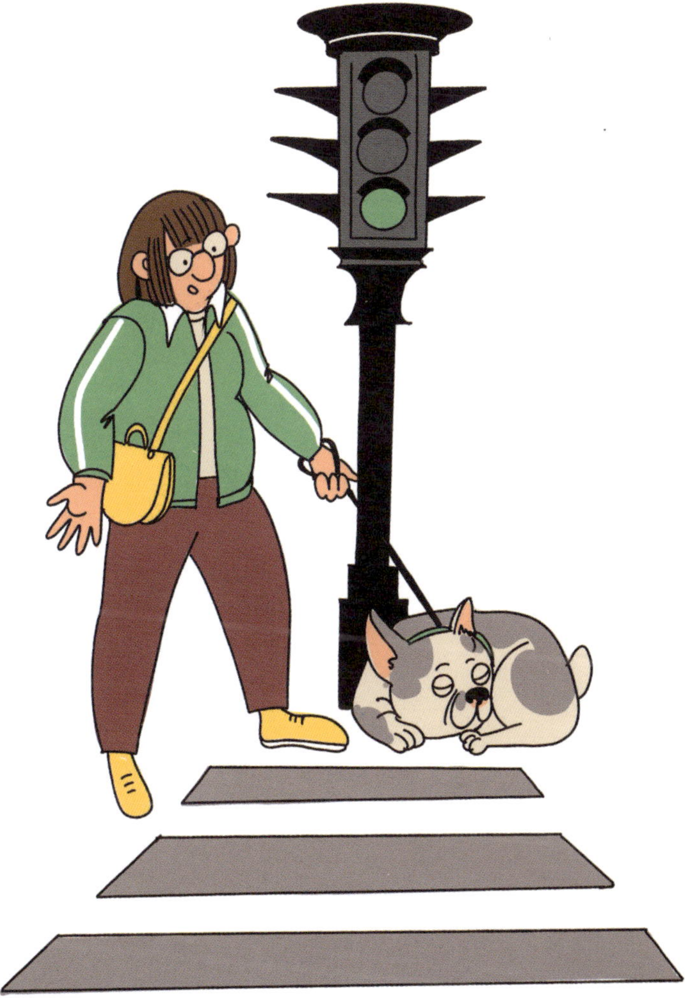

Your dog may look
for their golden
opportunity to help
you in the garden.

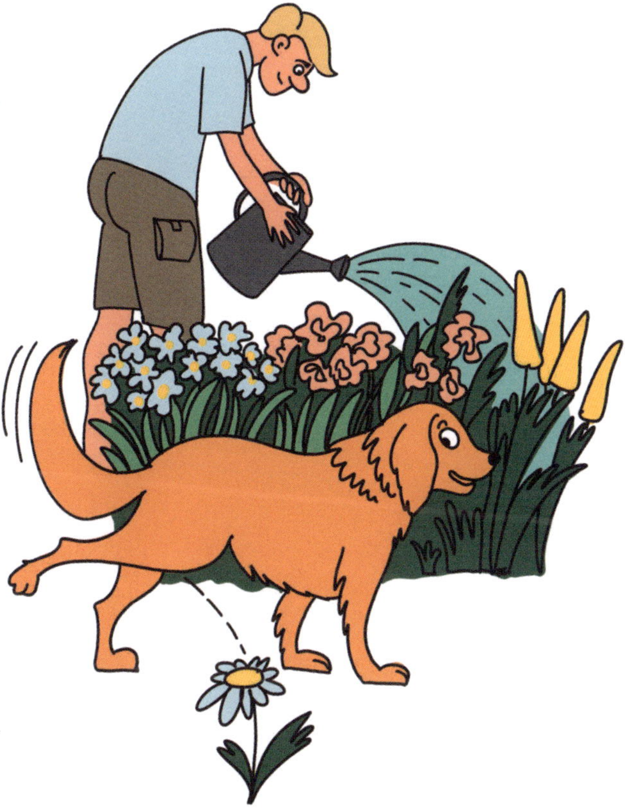

In an effort to
be helpful, your dog
will always make it
clear when they need
to go outside.

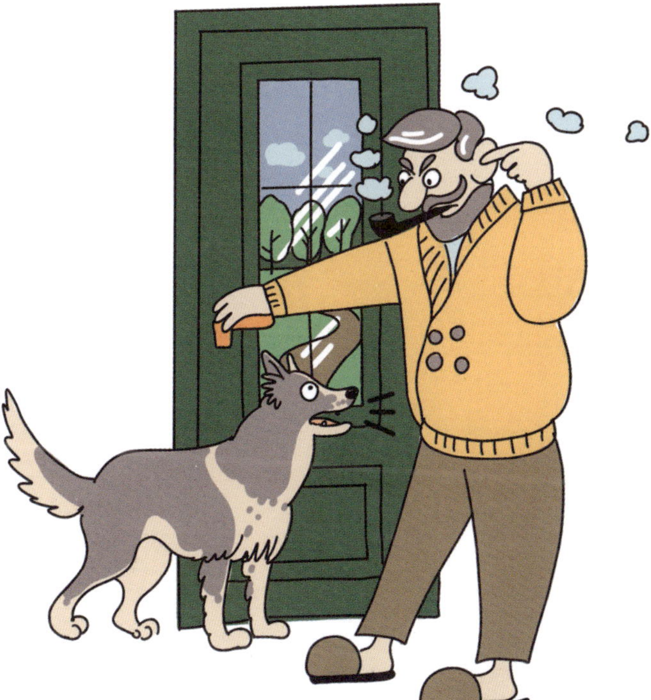

Your pup will be
careful not to leave
you on your own
for too long.

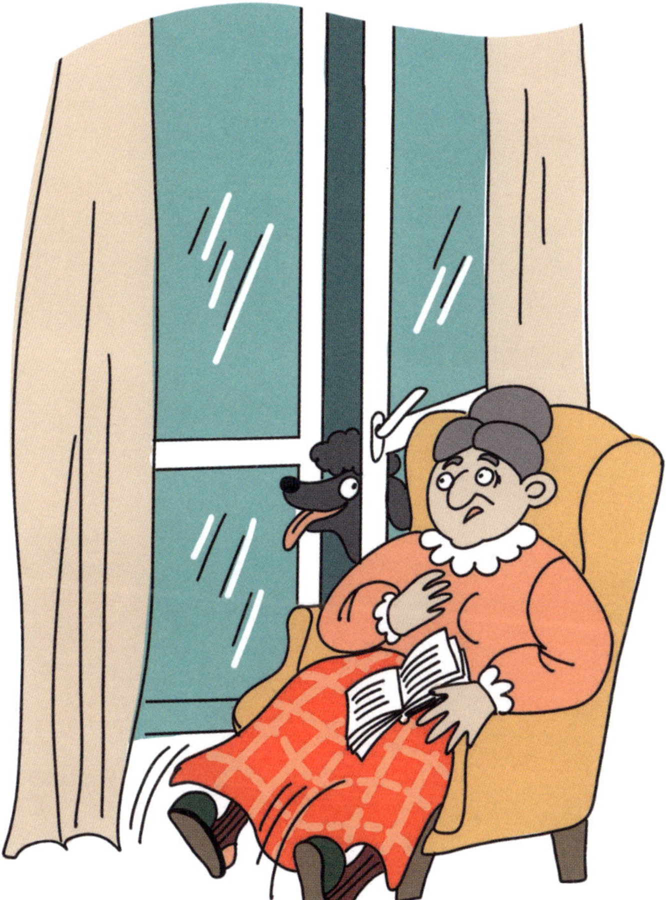

With all the love and
care you give them,
don't be surprised if your
dog thinks you'd be thrilled
to have even more pets.

Dogs will do their
best to respect your rules,
but keep in mind that
"no sitting on the furniture"
does leave some room
for ingenuity.

Just bought a new rug?
Your dog will be happy
to test it out for you.

Unsure whether your food is cool enough to eat yet? Your dog will check that for you.

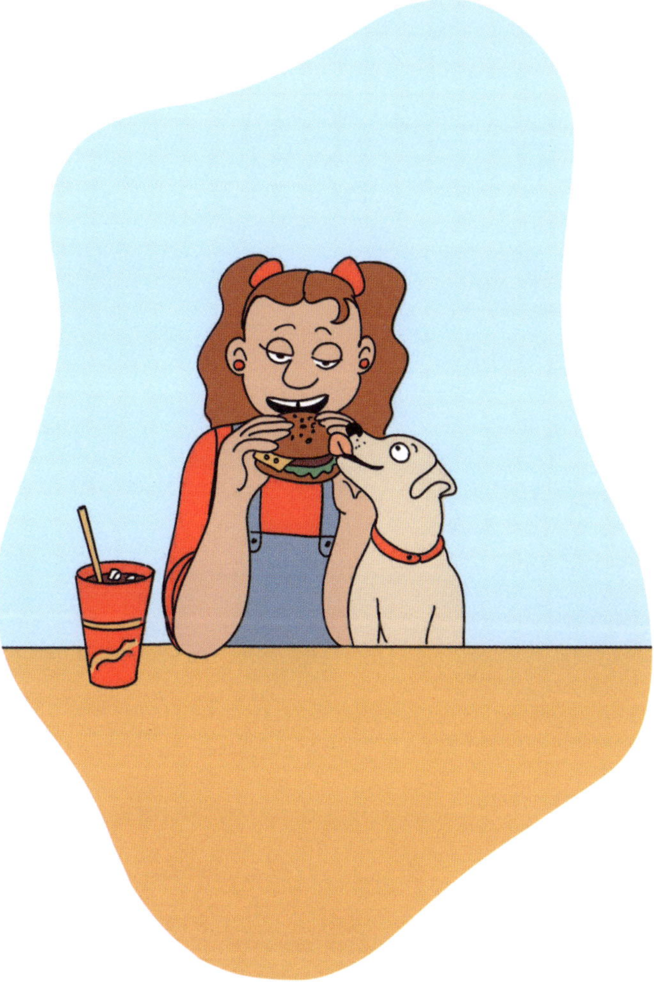

No matter what
they do, know that
your dog's actions
come from the heart.

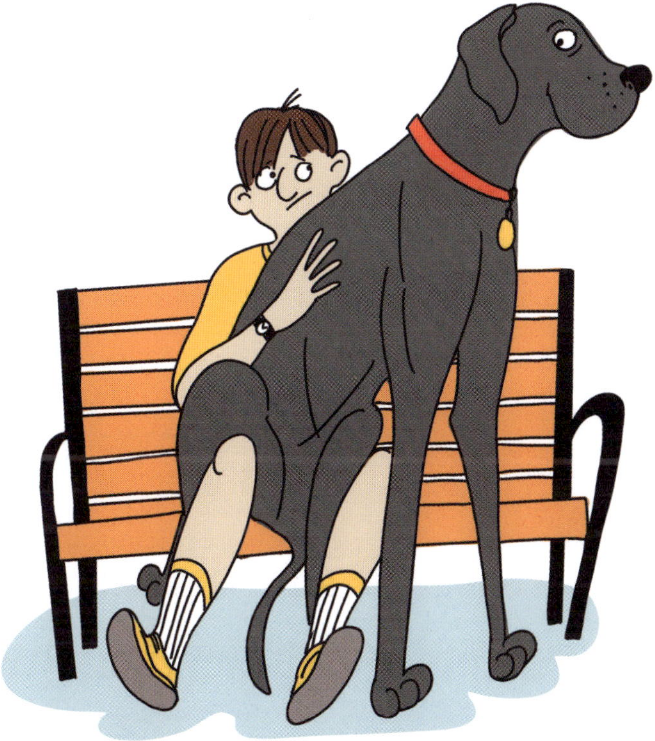

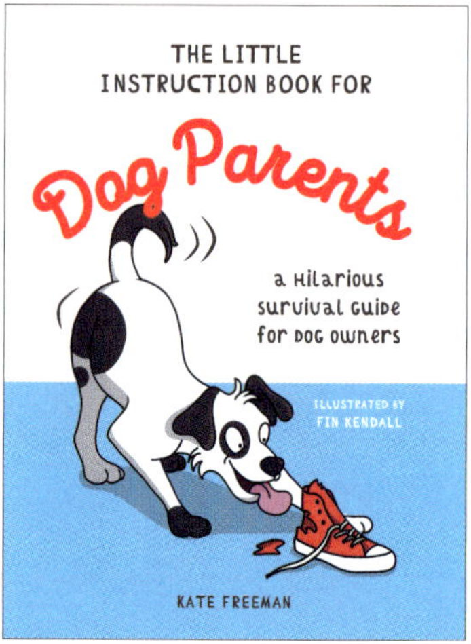
THE LITTLE
INSTRUCTION BOOK FOR
Dog Parents
a Hilarious
survival guide
for dog owners
ILLUSTRATED BY
FIN KENDALL
KATE FREEMAN

The Little Instruction Book for Dog Parents: A Hilarious Survival Guide for Dog Owners

Written by Kate Freeman
Illustrated by Fin Kendall

Hardback | 978-1-83799-364-2

This hilarious, no-nonsense survival guide is on hand to help you accept that being a dog parent is not a choice, but a lifestyle. Filled with original illustrations and tongue-in-cheek advice, this sneak peek into the world behind those puppy-dog eyes will make the perfect gift for any dog lover.

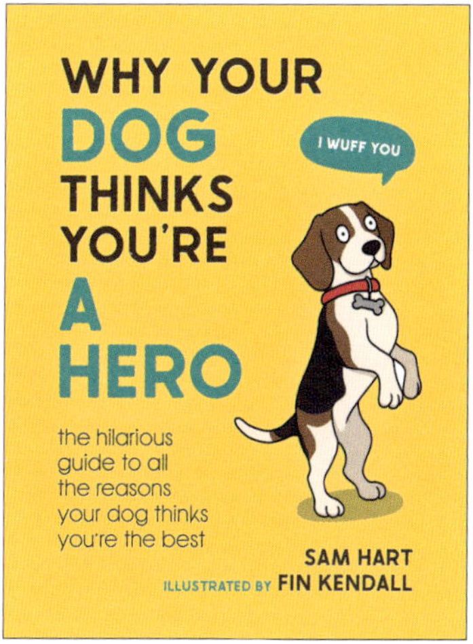
WHY YOUR
DOG
THINKS
YOU'RE
A
HERO
I WUFF YOU
the hilarious
guide to all
the reasons
your dog thinks
you're the best
SAM HART
ILLUSTRATED BY FIN KENDALL

Why Your Dog Thinks You're a Hero: The Hilarious Guide to All the Reasons Your Dog Thinks You're the Best

Written by Sam Hart
Illustrated by Fin Kendall

Hardback | 978-1-80007-931-1

Filled with witty original illustrations, this book explains the curious reasons behind all your dog's goofy looks and behaviours. Discover what your dog is saying through their barks and tail wags, and why they think you're the best.

Have you enjoyed this book?
If so, find us on Facebook at **Summersdale Publishers**, on Twitter/X at **@Summersdale** and on Instagram and TikTok at **@summersdalebooks** and get in touch. We'd love to hear from you!

www.summersdale.com